ISAAC ASIMOV'S NEW LIBRARY OF THE UNIVERSE

THE 21ST CENTURY IN SPACE

BY ISAAC ASIMOV and ROBERT GIRAUD

WITH REVISIONS AND UPDATING BY GREG WALZ-CHOJNACKI

Gareth Stevens Publishing

MILWAUKEE

For a free color catalog describing Gareth Stevens' list of high-quality books, call 1-800-542-2595 (USA) or 1-800-461-9120 (Canada). Gareth Stevens' Fax: (414) 225-0377.

Library of Congress Cataloging-in-Publication Data

Asimov, Isaac.
  The 21st century in space / by Isaac Asimov and Robert Giraud; with revisions and updating by Greg Walz-Chojnacki.
      p. cm. — (Isaac Asimov's New library of the universe)
  Rev. ed. of: The future in space. 1993.
  Includes index.
  Summary: Projects astronomical and astronautical possibilities for the the future, such as huge telescopes, airplanes in space, a probe to the sun, and a landing on Mars.
  ISBN 0-8368-1294-8
  1. Space sciences—Juvenile literature. 2. Astronomy—Juvenile literature.
3. Astronautics in astronomy—Juvenile literature. [1. Space sciences.
2. Astronomy. 3. Astronautics. 4. Forecasting.] I. Walz-Chojnacki, 1954-.
II. Asimov, Isaac. The future in space. III. Title. IV. Series: Asimov, Isaac.
New library of the universe.
QB500.22.A4513 1996
500.5—dc20   95-40362

This edition first published in 1996 by
Gareth Stevens Publishing
1555 North RiverCenter Drive, Suite 201
Milwaukee, Wisconsin 53212, USA

Project editor: Barbara J. Behm
Design adaptation: Helene Feider
Editorial assistant: Diane Laska
Production director: Teresa Mahsem
Picture research: Père Castor Flammarion and Diane Laska

Printed in the United States of America

1 2 3 4 5 6 7 8 9 99 98 97 96

To bring this classic of young people's information up to date, the editors at Gareth Stevens Publishing have selected two noted science authors, Greg Walz-Chojnacki and Francis Reddy. Walz-Chojnacki and Reddy coauthored the recent book *Celestial Delights: The Best Astronomical Events Through 2001*.

Walz-Chojnacki is also the author of the book *Comet: The Story Behind Halley's Comet* and various articles about the space program. He was an editor of *Odyssey*, an astronomy and space technology magazine for young people, for eleven years.

Reddy is the author of nine books, including *Halley's Comet, Children's Atlas of the Universe, Children's Atlas of Earth Through Time*, and *Children's Atlas of Native Americans*, plus numerous articles. He was an editor of *Astronomy* magazine for several years.

CONTENTS

We live in an enormously large place – the Universe. It's just in the last fifty-five years or so that we've found out how large it probably is. It's only natural that we would want to understand the place in which we live, so scientists have developed instruments – such as radio telescopes, satellites, probes, and many more – that have told us far more about the Universe than could possibly be imagined.

We have seen planets up close. We have learned about quasars and pulsars, black holes, and supernovas. We have gathered amazing data about how the Universe may have come into being and how it may end. Nothing could be more astonishing.

Scientists around the world are working tirelessly in the endless advancement of space technology. More and more space vehicles piloted by men and women who have strong spirits of adventure are launched each year. What discoveries, what technical achievements will we witness in the years to come in the continuous unfolding of human space exploration?

Isaac Asimov

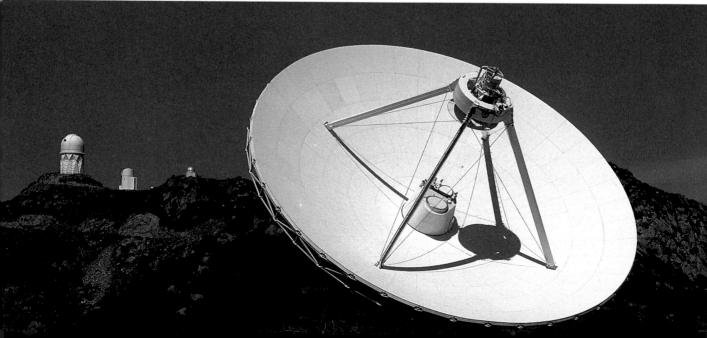

The Scope of Telescopes

Ancient peoples had no hope of getting a close view of the stars. It was only with Galileo Galilei's telescope in 1609 and Sir Isaac Newton's telescope seventy years later that modern astronomy was born.

A telescope works because of a mirror, or lens, that gathers and focuses light. The larger the mirror, the better and clearer the image. The largest mirror in a telescope is in the Zelenchukskaya telescope in the former Soviet Union. This telescope's mirror is 236 inches (6 meters) in diameter. It was completed in 1976. A new telescope currently being built in Chile will break this record. This telescope is called the VLT (Very Large Telescope). Each of its four mirrors measures 315 inches (8 m) across.

The best of what are known as the multiple-mirror telescopes is the Keck telescope in the Hawaiian Islands. Its 36 mirrors of 71 inches (1.8 m) each combine to form a single mirror of 394 inches (10 m). It will soon have a twin, Keck II, making the Keck system even more powerful.

Opposite, top: A quadruple telescope, the VLT, is under construction in Chile.

Opposite, bottom: One of the antennae of the VLBA network of radio telescopes located in Arizona is pictured.

The Universe in All "Colors"

We only see the Universe in the colors of visible light. But there is a lot more to the sky than that. Starting with the first radio telescopes in the 1920s, astronomers began to examine the sky in "invisible" wavelengths of light – from the long waves of radio to the short waves of X rays and gamma rays.

Earth's atmosphere blocks short wavelengths, so X ray, gamma ray, and ultraviolet astronomy must be undertaken from space. Because Earth's atmosphere "bubbles" like a pot of boiling water, even regular visible light astronomy is improved when the viewing is done from above the atmosphere.

Beginning with the Hubble Space Telescope, a series of "Great Observatories" in space is being developed. These instruments are operated by remote control from Earth.

Below: The Advanced X ray Astronomical Facility (AXAF) will be able to capture X rays in space to indicate the location of black holes.

Opposite, top: The Compton Gamma Ray Observatory was launched in 1991. It will study the Sun and quasars.

Opposite, bottom, left: The Space Infrared Telescope Facility (SIRTF) will be launched in 2001. It will study dark objects that are too cool to emit visible light, such as comets and newborn stars.

Opposite, bottom, right: The Hubble Space Telescope, the first of the Great Observatories in space, is already presenting sharper views of the Universe than ever seen before. Its position above the atmosphere gives the Hubble an enormous advantage over telescopes on Earth.

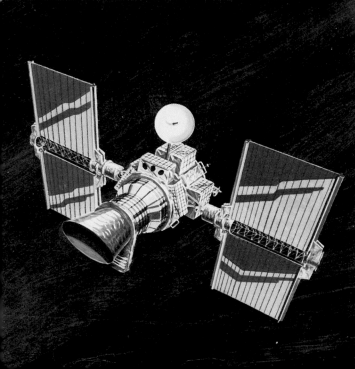
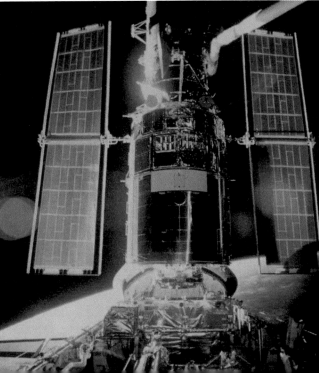

LIGO: A New Brand of Astronomy

Examining the skies in various invisible wavelengths of light revolutionized our understanding of the Universe. Now a new revolution is beginning.

Scientists have begun constructing a pair of detectors to search for gravity waves. Astronomers believe gravity waves are created whenever huge amounts of matter – like stars – are violently shaken or moved.

The Laser Interferometric Gravitational-Wave Observatory, or LIGO, is designed to detect the tiny ripples in space created by violent galactic explosions.

Whenever a new way of observing the Universe is developed, surprising and important new facts about the Universe are revealed. Astronomers believe that many new and unexpected discoveries will be made with the use of LIGO.

Below: LIGO is designed to detect tiny ripples, or waves, in the actual fabric of space. The ripples are so small that laser beams 2.2 miles (3.5 kilometers) long will be needed to measure them.

Opposite: The stupendous stellar explosions called supernovas produce gravity waves. Supernovas often create black holes, which LIGO may also be able to examine.

?*A new way to launch rockets?*

Rockets fly in space where there is no oxygen. But rocket engines need oxygen to work within Earth's atmosphere. Airplanes also need oxygen in order for their engines to operate. Suppose rockets were launched from airplanes to somehow combine the efforts of both. Would it work? On April 5, 1990, the United States rocket Pegasus *was flown to a height of 42,650 feet (13,000 m) by an airplane.* Pegasus *then detached and fired a charge that successfully launched it into orbit.*

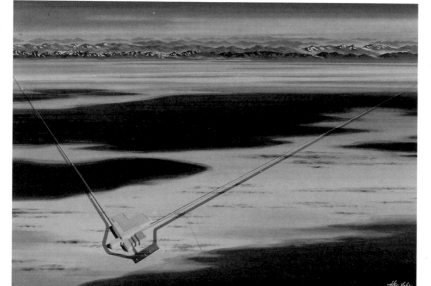

Transatmospheric Airplanes

! **Mariner 10** *and a*
mission to the Moon!

Mariner *refers to a series of*
U. S. space probes that has
provided information about
Mercury, Venus, Mars, and
more. Due to Mariner 10*'s*
many discoveries, scientists
from the United States,
Europe, and Japan are
organizing a joint mission
to the Moon.

The traditional rocket may someday be replaced by an airplane called the transatmospheric airplane. This airplane could thrust itself into space from a horizontal takeoff position. To do this, it would use oxygen from the air until it reaches an altitude of 15 miles (25 km). After that, it would use oxygen stored in its tanks.

In 1986, the United States began work on the *NASP*, or *X30*, an experimental aircraft designed to fly at the high speed necessary to reach outer space. France is working on the *AGV*, or *Avion à Grande Vitesse* (Airplane of Great Speed). This vehicle will be able to transport 150 passengers at a speed of more than 3,100 miles (5,000 km) per hour to an altitude of 19 miles (30 km). The German *Sänger* project and the British *HOTOL* (Horizontal Takeoff and Landing) project will result in airplanes that are able to reach orbit. These planes will fly through the air at high speed until they enter outer space. They will return to the ground like ordinary airplanes. They are being designed to carry passengers as well as cargo.

? *Propulsion in*
outer space?

Different types of propulsion
are available for use in outer
space. Rocket chemical
engines are powered by the
reaction of fuel and oxygen.
Ionic engines can attain
considerable speed but are
not very powerful. Nuclear
energy in the form of nuclear-
thermics is also available.
However, this type of pro-
pulsion poses a potential
danger to the environment.

Opposite, top: An immense sail, a vehicle in space, travels toward its destination. *Inset:* An illustration of what a transatmospheric airplane might look like.

Opposite, bottom, left: The French project *AGV*, or *Avion à Grande Vitesse* (Airplane of Great Speed).

Opposite, bottom, right: Britain's space airplane, *HOTOL*, is seen traveling on top of its huge transporter, *Autonov-225*.

11

Space Station Cooperatives

Scientists conduct many types of experiments to gather information about space. For example, they are testing the ability of the human body to withstand interplanetary flights lasting several years. Tests of this type need to be conducted at space stations. But space stations are too expensive for any one country to operate alone. Therefore, several countries are combining their efforts.

Alpha is a large international space station composed of independent modules, or units. One module belongs to the United States, one to Europe, and one to Japan. In the near future, these modules will connect with each other in space.

Right: A drawing of the orbital unit *Columbus* at the space station *Alpha*.

! *Women in astronomy!*

More and more women are becoming leaders in the field of astronomy, a field long dominated by men. Heidi Hammel is a team leader for Hubble Space Telescope observations. Reta Beebe is one of the world's top experts on the cloud structure of Jupiter. Imke de Pater set up a network of radio observatories in the U.S., Europe, and Australia. Carolyn Shoemaker, along with her husband Eugene, and colleague David Levy, discovered the Shoemaker-Levy 9 comet. So far, Carolyn Shoemaker has discovered 32 comets, more than any other living person. For a future in astronomy, girls and boys should take as many math and physics classes as possible. Youngsters should observe the night sky, and read all the books and magazines available about astronomy.

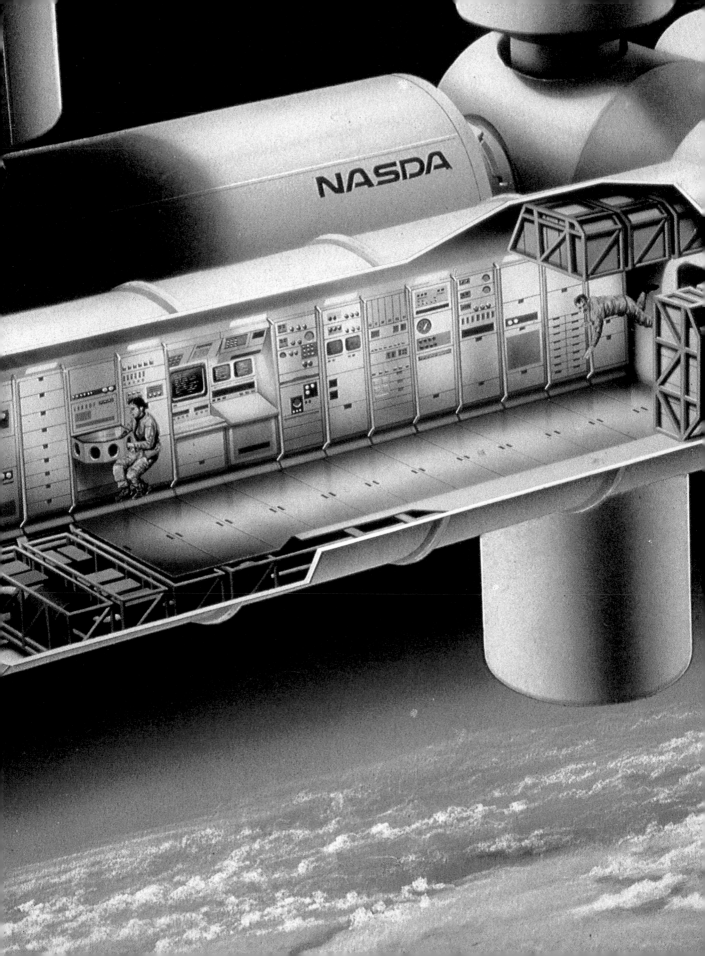

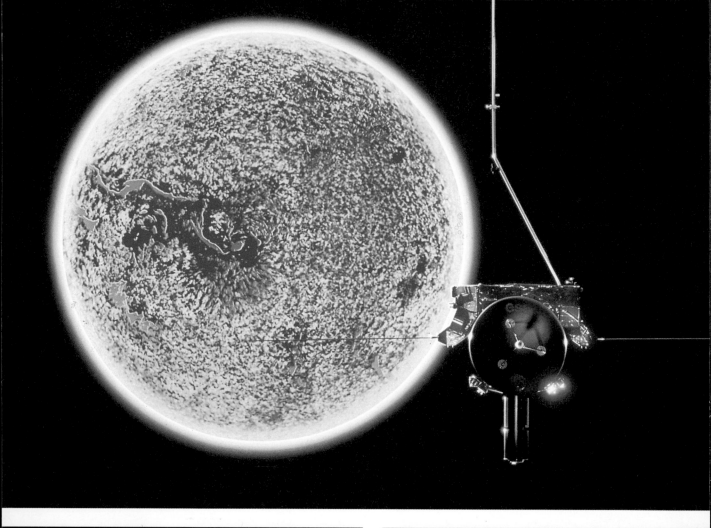

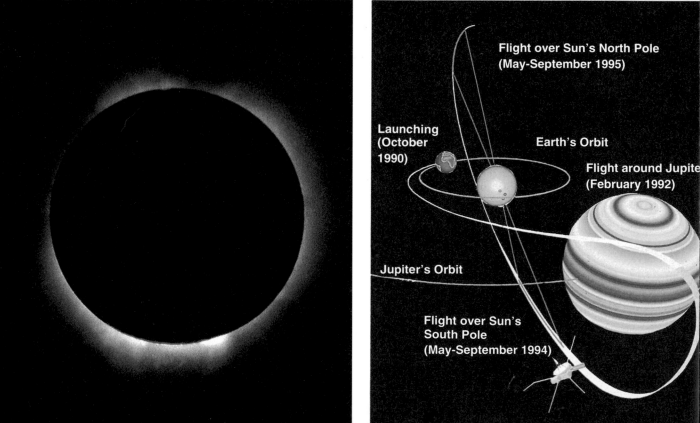

Flight over Sun's North Pole
(May-September 1995)

Launching
(October
1990)

Earth's Orbit

Flight around Jupite
(February 1992)

Jupiter's Orbit

Flight over Sun's
South Pole
(May-September 1994)

Sun Studies

The Sun is the only star that may be within our reach. As on other stars, violent and abundant phenomena occur on the Sun's surface. These phenomena, for the most part, have nothing in common with the types of activity that occur on Earth's surface.

The European space probe *Ulysses*, launched in 1990, is the first probe to fly over the poles of the Sun. Matter and radiation are less affected by the rotation and magnetic field of the Sun at the poles.

The European Space Agency (ESA) has an orbital observatory called *Soho* used for the study of the Sun. *Soho* carries scientific instruments such as spectrometers, telescopes, and a coronograph. *Soho* has the ability to detect small oscillations of solar matter, during which the photosphere (the part of the Sun visible to us) "rings" like a bell.

In the shade of the Moon!

The part of the Sun we can see is the photosphere. Above the photosphere are the fainter chromosphere and corona. These outer layers are usually lost in the brilliant glow of the photosphere. During what is known as a total solar eclipse, the Moon completely covers the photosphere. This makes it possible to see the outer regions of the Sun's atmosphere. Total solar eclipses occur only once or twice a year somewhere on Earth. On July 11, 1991, one of the world's best-equipped observatories, located at Mauna Kea in Hawaii, found itself in the shady zone of the Moon, allowing a clear view of the chromosphere and corona.

Living Beyond Earth

Mars has fascinated people for a long time. Exploring this planet promises to be the great space event of the first part of the twenty-first century. The United States has made plans to extensively explore this planet to get ready for visits by humans. Unfortunately, the first step in the plan, the Mars *Observer* spacecraft, failed shortly before reaching the Red Planet in 1993. A replacement spacecraft, Mars *Surveyor*, is set for launch in 1996. While Mars *Surveyor* maps the planet from orbit, the Mars *Pathfinder* rover will drop down to the planet. There it will explore the surface of Mars. Beginning in 1996, NASA plans to send two probes every two years to Mars for ten years.

Closer to home, NASA is working on a *Lunar Prospector* mission that will orbit and map the surface of Earth's Moon for up to three years.

Opposite, top: After the Moon, the second celestial body humans will visit is Mars.

Opposite, bottom, right: A Russian vehicle scheduled to travel to Mars is capable of carrying a load of 110-220 pounds (50-100 kg). It will land on Mars in 1996.

Below, left: The *Lunar Prospector* will map all of the Moon's surface. Special detectors will indicate the type of minerals the lunar soil contains. Such knowledge will be important in planning permanent settlements on the Moon.

Below, center: Scientists will someday observe Mars from Phobos, a moon of Mars.

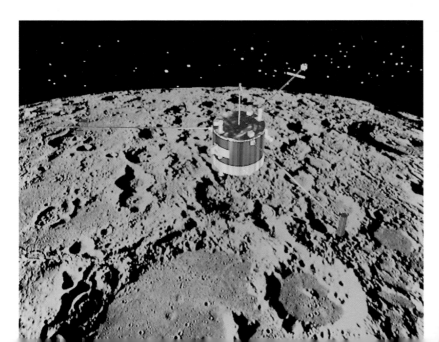

GALILEO

Flights over Earth
(December 1990 & December 1992)

Flight over Venus
(February 1990)

**Earth
Launching**
(October 1989)

Ida
(August 1993)

Jupiter's Orbit

Gaspra
(October 1991)

Arrival
(December 7, 1995)

Probing Jupiter

Launched in October 1989, the U.S. space probe *Galileo* has so far passed near Venus in February 1990 and Earth in December 1990 and December 1992. On October 29, 1991, at a distance of only 995 miles (1,600 km) away, it began the first survey of an asteroid (Gaspra) ever performed by a probe.

Galileo's orbiter is scheduled to circle Jupiter for twenty months beginning in December 1995. Another probe will then be released into the depths of Jupiter's atmosphere. This probe should be able to take measurements for at least one hour before being destroyed by the high temperature and pressure that exist in the depths of Jupiter's atmosphere.

Top: The probe *Galileo*, placed by an artist on a photo of Jupiter.

Opposite, bottom, left: Unlike on Earth, a straight line in space is not the shortest route between points.

Opposite, bottom, right: The first close-up of an asteroid, Gaspra, as seen by *Galileo* in 1991.

? Can Galileo be fixed?

Galileo's main antenna failed to open as planned shortly after launch. This antenna is necessary to send pictures and data back to Earth from Jupiter. NASA's engineers have experience fixing spacecraft that are millions of miles from Earth. One way to open the antenna is to turn the craft back and forth, hoping the change from cold to hot (caused by sunlight) will loosen the antenna. Another plan is to quickly start and stop the antenna motor to "hammer" the antenna open. Galileo has a smaller antenna that still works, but it is weaker than the main antenna and can send only a portion of the information.

Cassini – Saturn's New Moon?

The launching of the U.S. probe *Cassini* in 1997 should begin one of the most exciting stages of the exploration of the Solar System. *Cassini* is an advanced space probe that will become an artificial satellite of the planet Saturn in 2005. On board will be the European probe *Huygens* that will aim toward the surface of Titan, a moon of Saturn. *Cassini* will circle Saturn at its ring system for four years. It will study in detail Saturn's rings, atmosphere, and magnetosphere (the zone influenced by its magnetic field). *Huygens* will analyze, in the course of its descent, the atmosphere of Titan. It will then either crash or sink into Titan's surface, depending on whether the surface is solid or liquid.

Right: In 1997, *Cassini* will undertake a four-year mission to Saturn to study the planet's rings, atmosphere, and magnetosphere.

Opposite, inset: The route *Cassini* will follow to reach Saturn.

! *The mysteries of Titan!*

Titan is the ninth largest body in the Solar System. Unlike all the other moons, it has a thick atmosphere. The probe Voyager *has located some organic compounds in Titan's atmosphere. Under certain conditions, the types of compounds found can generate living matter. Titan's surface, hidden by the thickness of its atmosphere, remains a puzzle. It is possible that it might be entirely or partially covered by an ocean of methane gas. The* Huygens *probe will reveal the answer to this mystery.*

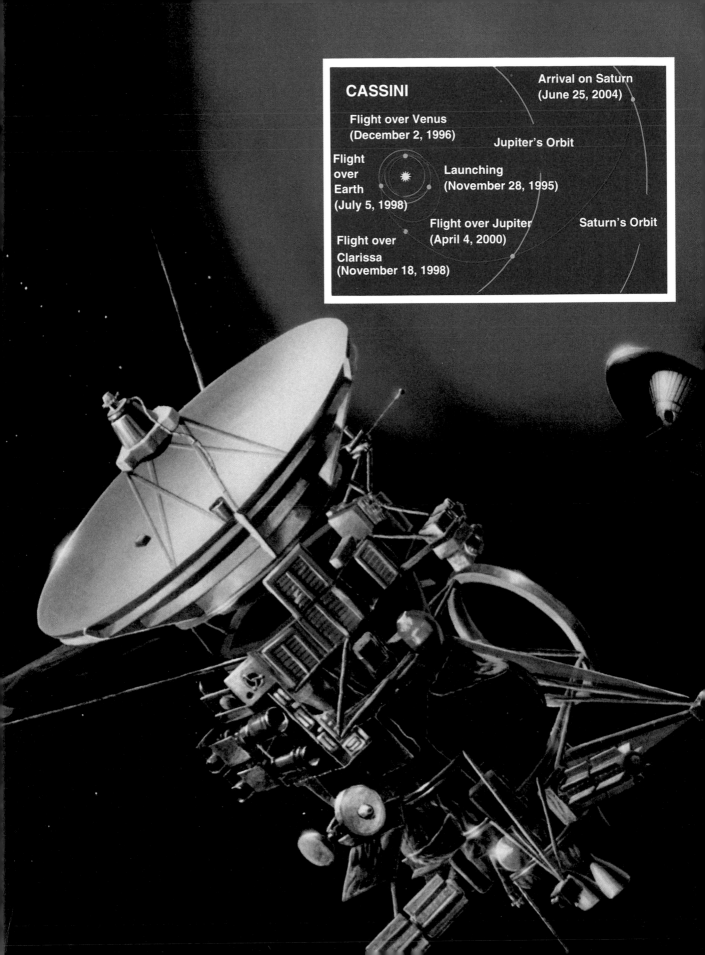

CASSINI

Arrival on Saturn
(June 25, 2004)

Flight over Venus
(December 2, 1996)

Jupiter's Orbit

Flight
over
Earth
(July 5, 1998)

Launching
(November 28, 1995)

Flight over Jupiter
(April 4, 2000)

Saturn's Orbit

Flight over
Clarissa
(November 18, 1998)

V 44

European Space Agency

! In limbo!

Russian cosmonaut Sergei Krikalev began his mission in space on May 18, 1991, orbiting Earth in the space station Mir. *He was to return home after just five months. During his third month in space, however, a coup was attempted in his country to preserve the communist government. The coup failed, and the former Soviet Union's space program was put on hold for financial reasons. This meant that Krikalev had to stay in space indefinitely. A rocket containing food and supplies was launched to him. Eventually, after 313 days in space, Krikalev was allowed to return to Earth.*

The European Space Agency (ESA) was created in 1975. Member countries of the organization include Germany, Austria, Belgium, Denmark, Spain, France, Ireland, Italy, Norway, Canada, the Netherlands, the United Kingdom, Sweden, and Switzerland. Finland is scheduled to join.

The ESA has built the booster *Ariane*, which will launch most civilian satellites. It has already successfully launched telecommunications, meteorological, and teledetection (for the study of terrestrial surfaces) satellites.

As a part of its program, the ESA is forming a corps of astronauts around Germany's Ulf Merbold, the Netherlands's Wubbo Ockels (both of whom have already participated in the ESA's and NASA's *Spacelab* missions), Belgium's Dirk Frimout, and Switzerland's Claude Nicollier. Only six astronauts were in the program in 1991, but the ESA is steadily building this number.

Opposite: The European Space Agency booster *Ariane* at the moment of firing.

Left: A Russian crew on board space station *Mir*.

A New Era of Exploration

Exciting space expeditions are now in the planning worldwide. One mission is called the Near Earth Asteroid Rendezvous *(NEAR)*. It will place a spacecraft in orbit around the asteroid Eros.

A mission called *Stardust* will gather materials from comets. The Venus *Multiprobe* Mission will send a fleet of sixteen small probes into Venus's thick atmosphere. Still another mission, *Suess-Urey*, will collect samples of the solar wind. *Pluto Express*, scheduled for launch in 2003, will send a pair of spacecraft to pay a call on the only planet never before visited by spacecraft from Earth.

All of these vehicles, which aren't much bigger than living room chairs, will reveal fascinating new information about our neighborhood in space.

Below, left: An artist's rendition of the *Stardust* mission. The mission, which could be launched in 1999, will pass near the Comet P/Wild 2 and capture comet material. The spacecraft will then return to Earth, where scientists will examine the comet matter.

Below, right: The *NEAR* spacecraft will orbit the asteroid Eros for a year, beginning in January 1999.

Opposite: The *Pluto Express* spacecraft will arrive at Pluto in 2010. Besides taking close-up pictures of the planet, it will send a Russian probe through Pluto's atmosphere. After flying past Pluto, it may move farther into the Kuiper Belt to explore this newly discovered realm.

Cosmic Soup

Scientists have found evidence that distant galaxies are rushing away from Earth at a higher speed than closer galaxies. In fact, the speed of the galaxies seems to be directly connected to their distances from Earth. This connection is one of the reasons most scientists accept the Big Bang theory of the formation of the Universe. According to this theory, the Universe began with a huge explosion that created a smooth, even "soup" of matter and energy. This "soup" became lumpy as stars, planets, and galaxies formed. Astronomers are currently trying to discover why these developments might have taken place.

Further, the huge assortment of instruments that scientists use to study space constantly uncovers new information. In 1991, scientists discovered signs pointing toward the existence of what might be the most gigantic of all the black holes. Black holes are areas in space with intensely strong gravitational fields.

The study of certain objects in space, such as black holes, may clear up many mysteries. For instance, the centers of galaxies seem to behave as though they are under the influence of masses of undetectable matter. Also, the velocity of stars at the heart of the galaxies does not seem to have a satisfactory explanation.

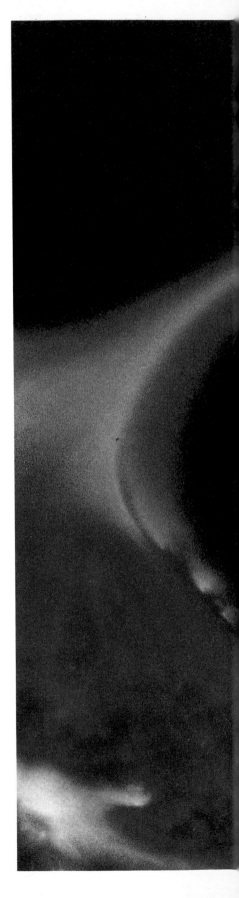

Discovering Extraterrestrial Life

If extraterrestrial life-forms do exist, they could survive nowhere but on planets. Innumerable planets probably exist in the Universe, but they are so faint in brightness when compared to the stars that they are difficult to detect and observe from Earth. Thanks to infrared telescopes, scientists have already located disks around stars. Planets may be forming – or already exist – in these disks. With ever-advancing technology, extrasolar planets may one day be discovered.

Far left: A black hole has a strong gravitational pull.

Left: The day when Earthlings will be able to fly over a distant planet is still far in the future.

The Future in Space

1995

December Launching of the European satellite *Cluster* to study the impact of the Sun on the particles and the magnetic field surrounding Earth.

Galileo arrives at Jupiter.

1996

Departure of the second Russian mission to Mars. Completion of the Keck II telescope in the Hawaiian Islands.

November Mars *Surveyor* launch.

December Mars *Pathfinder* launch.

1997

July Mars *Pathfinder* arrives.

October Launching of *Cassini*.

1998

Permanent occupation of the space station *Alpha*, including the habitable *Columbus* module.

Launching of the American X ray observatory AXAF.

1999-2000

Satellite reconnaissance envoy prepares for U.S. Moon arrival.

Launching of the European X ray observatory XXMM (ESA).

NEAR mission at Eros.

Stardust mission launched.

2000

Cassini flies over and surveys Jupiter.

Completion of the large telescope VLT with its four mirrors. It will have the equivalent of a single 53-foot (16-m) mirror, the largest and most powerful ever used by astronomers.

2001

Departure toward Mars of the first of the four American mini-laboratories *Mesur*. The second will follow in 2002, and the two final ones will depart in 2005.

Launch of SIRTF.

2002

The probe *Huygens* (*Cassini* mission) should descend toward Titan.

2003

Launching of the *Rosetta* mission.

The European shuttle *Hermès* will carry its first three astronauts.

The independent module of the European space station *Columbus* will perform its first mission.

Pluto Express launched.

Between 2003 and 2005

NASA anticipates the installation of an automatic experimental factory for the exploration of lunar resources, then the launching of six astronauts who will spend fourteen days on the Moon.

2008

Arrival of *Rosetta* on a comet to gather samples.

2010

Following the appraisals of NASA, the installation of twelve people on the Moon.

Pluto Express spacecraft makes closest approach to Pluto.

Between 2012 and 2014

According to NASA's plans, the unloading of necessary supplies on Mars.

2016

The most probable date, after NASA's calculations, for the Mars landing.

in 20,000 years

The probes *Voyager 1* and *Voyager 2* (launched in 1977) will travel across the Oort Cloud located at the extreme limits of the Solar System.

in 40,000 years

Voyager 1 will pass within 1.6 light-years of a star in the giraffe constellation Camelopardalis, about three light-years from Earth.

in 296,000 years

Voyager 2 will find itself in the distant suburbs of Sirius, the brightest star in the heavens, 8.6 light-years away from Earth.

More Books about Future Space Exploration

Distance Flights. Berliner (Lerner)
Journey to the Outer Planets. Barker (Rourke)
The NOVA Space Explorer's Guide: Where to Go and What to See. Maurer (Clarkson N. Potter)
Passage to Space: The Shuttle Transport System. Coombs (William Morrow)
Space Exploration and Travel. Sabin (Troll Associates)
Space Station. Apfel (Franklin Watts)
Space Travel. A Technological Frontier. DeOld and Judge (Davis Mass)

Videos

Mars: Our Mysterious Neighbor. (Gareth Stevens)
Our Milky Way and Other Galaxies. (Gareth Stevens)

Places to Visit

You can learn more about the future in space without leaving Earth. Here are some museums and centers where you can find a variety of space exhibits.

Air and Space Museum
Smithsonian Institution
601 Independence Avenue SW
Washington, D.C. 20560

Astrocentre
Royal Ontario Museum
100 Queen's Park
Toronto, Ontario M5S 2C6

International Women's Air and Space Museum
1 Chamber Plaza
Dayton, OH 45402

Henry Crown Science Center
Museum of Science and Industry
57th Street and Lake Shore Drive
Chicago, IL 60637

Anglo-Australian Observatory
Private Bag
Coonarbariban 2357
Australia

Palomar Observatory
35899 Canfield Road
Palomar Mountain, CA 92060

Places to Write

Here are some places to write for more information about the future in space. Be sure to state what kind of information you would like. Include your full name and address so they can write back to you.

National Space Society
922 Pennsylvania Avenue SE
Washington, D.C. 20003

Canadian Space Agency
Communications Department
6767 Route de L'Aeroport
Saint Hubert, Quebec J3Y 8Y9

Sydney Observatory
P.O. Box K346
Haymarket 2000 Australia

NASA Lewis Research Center
Educational Services Office
21000 Brookpark Road
Cleveland, OH 44135

Glossary

asteroids: very small planets, and even smaller objects made of rock or metal. There are thousands of asteroids in our Solar System. Most can be found orbiting the Sun in large numbers between Mars and Jupiter. But some show up elsewhere in our Solar System – some as meteoroids and some possibly as "captured" moons of planets, such as Mars.

atmosphere: the gaseous mass that surrounds a planet, moon, or star.

black hole: a massive object in space thought to be formed by the explosion and collapse of a star. The object is so dense that even light cannot escape the incredible force of its gravity.

booster: a solid fuel rocket used to help space vehicles lift off. A booster is also referred to as a solid rocket.

infrared: a ray with a wavelength that is just beyond the red end of the visible spectrum of light. Infrared rays are used to obtain pictures of objects in space that are obscured by haze in the atmosphere. Visible light is scattered by haze, but infrared rays are not.

magnetosphere: the zone surrounding a planet that is influenced by its magnetic field.

NASA: the National Aeronautics and Space Administration. NASA is the agency of the United States government that plans and operates space flights and exploration.

observatory: a building or other structure designed for observing and recording celestial movements and events.

orbit: the path that an object follows around a planet or star. An object can remain in orbit without relying on engine power because the force of gravity pulls it toward the planet or star.

photosphere: the luminous surface layer of the Sun or another star.

probe: a spacecraft that photographs and records data about celestial bodies. Sometimes probes even land on these bodies.

quasar: a very distant and luminous object found at the center of a galaxy.

satellite: an object that orbits another object in space. A moon is a natural satellite, while weather satellites or communications satellites are artificial satellites.

space station: a well-equipped laboratory that allows scientists to live and carry out research in space over long periods of time.

spectrometer: an instrument that measures the wave-lengths of images formed by rays of light or other radiation or sound.

telescope: an instrument that uses an arrangement of lenses, or mirrors, in a long tube to make objects that are far away appear closer.

ultraviolet: a ray with a wavelength just beyond the violet end of the visible spectrum of light. The Sun produces a large amount of ultraviolet light, but most of it is absorbed in the ozone layer, an area in the upper atmosphere of Earth.

Index

Born in 1920, Isaac Asimov came to the United States as a young boy from his native Russia. As a young man, he was a student of biochemistry. In time, he became one of the most productive writers the world has ever known. His books cover a spectrum of topics, including science, history, language theory, fantasy, and science fiction. His brilliant imagination gained him the respect and admiration of adults and children alike. Sadly, Isaac Asimov died shortly after the publication of the first edition of *Isaac Asimov's Library of the Universe.*

The publishers wish to thank the following for permission to reproduce copyright material: front cover, © European Space Agency (ESA); 4 (upper), © L. Bret/Sky and Space; 4 (lower), © S. Brunier/Sky and Space; 6, NASA; 7 (upper), © Michael Carroll; 7 (lower left), NASA; 7 (lower right), NASA/STScI; 8, Courtesy LIGO Project; 9, © Michael Carroll; 10 (upper), © Manchu/Sky and Space; 10 (center), © NASA/Sky and Space; 10 (lower left), © Aerospace; 10 (lower right), 12-13, 14 (upper), © European Space Agency (ESA); 14 (lower left), © S. Brunier/Sky and Space; 14 (lower right), © ESA/Sky and Space; 16, NASA; 16-17, © D. Hardy/Sky and Space; 17 (upper), © L. Bret/Sky and Space; 17 (lower), IKI/Sky and Space; 18 (left), © Sky and Space; 18 (right), © JPL/Sky and Space; 18-19, © NASA/Sky and Space; 20-21 (large), Jet Propulsion Laboratory; 21 (inset), © Sky and Space; 22, © ESA/CNES; 23, CNES/Glavcosmos; 24, Jet Propulsion Laboratory; 24-25, John Hopkins University; 25, © Michael Carroll; 26-27, © Mark Paternostro 1988; 27, © Doug McLeod 1988.